Caged

Caged
Again

Daarkie
Nightglare

Daarkie
Nightglare

If I were to fly away,
Where would I fly, anyway?
If I were to live my life in cage,
I wouldn't mind the change.

If noone bothered me all the time,
As life only gave me lemons and lime,
I would like to be in touch with few,
And everyday get book or two.

It does not need to be the cage of gold,
As long as it'd be warm and bold,
And big enough, I have my standards,
Though just to keep away any hazards.

I'd change painful freedom I've got,
For everything in cage, why not?
Because...
Because I don't have freedom anyway...

Daarkie Nightglare

Circles and circles are all around,
Tell me 'bout something that can't be
found.
Like honestly, truth, and glorious way,
Or the devil, evil, good, and grey.

Circles and circles are all around,
Tell me' bout something that can't be
found.
Like soul, language and the relationship,
All together on one great sinking ship.

Circles and circles are all around,
Tell me 'bout something that can't be found,
The perfect circle, line, or the pi,
All hidden in a shepherd' s pie.

Circles and circles are all around,
Now show me something that I can find,
The amber sunset in amber autumn,
And this poem, its unclear bottom.

Daarkie

Nightglare

Daarkie Nightglare

In the midst of the darkness,
Holding my last breath,
As sad and so evil,
As the devil aways was,
I know river I cannot pass,
For I never talked to the devil,
Even though we've met,
I didn't pretend loneliness.

And there are things I cannot share,
Things I live with, now,
But that's all I have, you know?
Don't forget, never let go,
And they ask me, how?
When my heart is not really there.

I let go of the fear of mine,
I am going to the river,
Which may be my only savior,
I don't go in straight line.

Let me fell to happiness,
With the river of forgetfulness.

EVERYTHING IS NOT
WHAT IT SEEMS, BUT
WHAT AM I SUPPOSED
TO BELIEVE IN?
I DON'T KNOW
ANYMORE.
SO... LET'S BELIEVE IN
OURSELVES.

Daarkie Nightglare

My lips with your
finger sealed,
Cannot tell the secret of
mine,
How much I need
being healed,
Not standing in the
line

How much do I need
some warming,
And loving welcome,
How much do I need
hugging,
And more kisses, and
some

I need you...

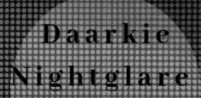

Daarkie
Nightglare

Happy birthday
to little me,
Happy birthday
to sweet me,
Happy birthday
to lonely me,
Happy birthday
to scared me.

Daarkie Nightglare

I got a rose of
blue,
It was nice, and
lovely too,
And if they are
asking who,...
I got it from
you.

It was so
pretty,
It made me
smile,
Not being
pity,
It'll last for a
while.

Daarkie
Nightglare

Hush, now, it's beginning,
With last drops of your innocence.
Hush, now, stop struggling,
Under the false pretense.

Hush, now, you are only toy,
As if you were ever meant to be more,
Hush, now, you are bit too coy,
For someone who is now my whore.

Hush, now, "no" is not a word,
You should be able to say.
Hush, now, for I've yet to heard,
You enjoying our little play.

Hush, now, it's over,
I just took my part
Hush, now, the sooner,
You get out, again we can start...

Daarkie Nightglare

Daarkie Nightglare

Stand on my feet, in the darkness surrounding me, I know I am failing to stay alive.

But I have to.

...

Right?

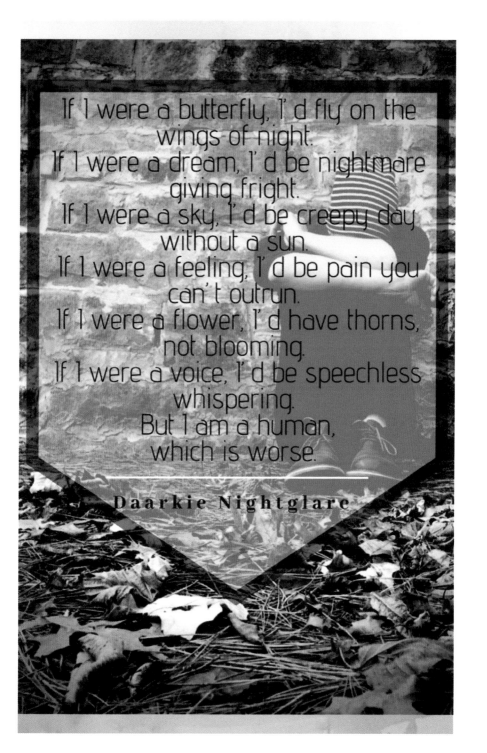

If I were a butterfly, I'd fly on the wings of night.
If I were a dream, I'd be nightmare giving fright.
If I were a sky, I'd be creepy day without a sun.
If I were a feeling, I'd be pain you can't outrun.
If I were a flower, I'd have thorns, not blooming.
If I were a voice, I'd be speechless whispering.
But I am a human,
which is worse.

Daarkie Nightglare

Even though he always knew it was supposed to happen, he never actually believed in it... Like, why would he, right? Life is so cruel and full of hatred...
And then he looked into her eyes.
She was smiling, in her own way.
She was smiling with her eyes.
She was gentle, she was loving, like an autumn color warm.
She, so warm and loving and gentle, with a smile offered her hand.
As he fell in love with angel, with darkest wings possible, he realized who she was.
She was there for him, for she was the Death.

Daarkie
Nightglare

Life without tomorrow,
Eyes without stain,

Eyes full of sorrow,
Life full of pain.

Daarkie Nightglare

Girl without past,
Boy without arm,

Boy full of lust,
Girl full of harm.

As if life was easy, as if life wasn't grey,
Let's see where it takes us, don't pray.
If he would exist, I would have to hate,
The one who always comes so late.

In my mind, for thought of you,
I may want to see the blue,
Of the raging, calming sea,
This is now, what I really see...

The surroundings, so different from the chaos,
In my head, such a way to find a loss,
Here, take my hand and take me,
Where I can let myself just be.

Daarkie
Nightglare

As autumn leaves fall to the ground,

I can not hear the silver sound,

As I am falling from within,

Praying he would let me in,

Reaching for his hand and heart,

Touching my own inner art,

I stand strong and unmoveable,

Let's make the amber light double,

As if our calming fiery show,

Wasn't shun down by the snow...

Daarkie Nightglare

If your life was a song, how would it go?

If your life was a lie, what would it say?

If your life was a kiss, how would it feel?

If your life was an angel, of what would be his wings?

If your life was a note, how would you sing?

If your life was a demon, what would be his sin?

If your life was a creature, where would it live?

If your life was a flower, which color would it take?

If your life was a power, what would it allow?

If your life was a cage, out of what would it be made?

If your life was a hero, who would he save?

If your life was an answer, what would be the question?

If your life was a precious stone, which one what it be?

If your life was a gift... What would you say?

Daarkie Nightglare

They say, that time heals. I don't feel healed at all, just the opposite. I am realizing, slowly, more and more, that I am a broken person inside. Time doesn't heal, it just gives us the ability to carry the pain.
And just as well, I feel pain... For I've killed. Others might have hurt her, but I killed her, in the end, unable to live with the one who used to be real and true. I killed the girl I used to be...
And now I am to pay the final price.

They say, that time heals.

Daarkie Nightglare

I wanted to draw a heart for you. But I didn't know which. I wanted to give you something. But I didn't know what. I wanted to tell you a lot of words. But I didn't know whose. I wanted to fly away. But I didn't know where. I wanted to make you feel better. But I didn't know how. I wanted to hear you say hi to me. But I didn't know when. I wanted to write this letter. Still I don't know why...

———————————————

Daarkie Nightglare

YOU FELL IN LOVE
WITH A GIRL
I USED TO BE...
BUT SHE'S DEAD.
YOU KILLED HER

Daarkie
Nightglare

I fell in love with a painting,

So warm, colorful and kind,

One look at his pose,

I am all dancing on toes,

Who said that love is blind?

I fell in love with a painting...

Daarkie Nightglare

My own
shadow,
Following me,
Is stronger
than me...
Not so
shallow.

And prettier.
(but still mine)

Daarkie Nightglare

Just a glimpse. That's all I need.
Just a glimpse of the future.
Just a glimpse of the truth.
Just... Reality.
And...

You

Daarkie Nightglare

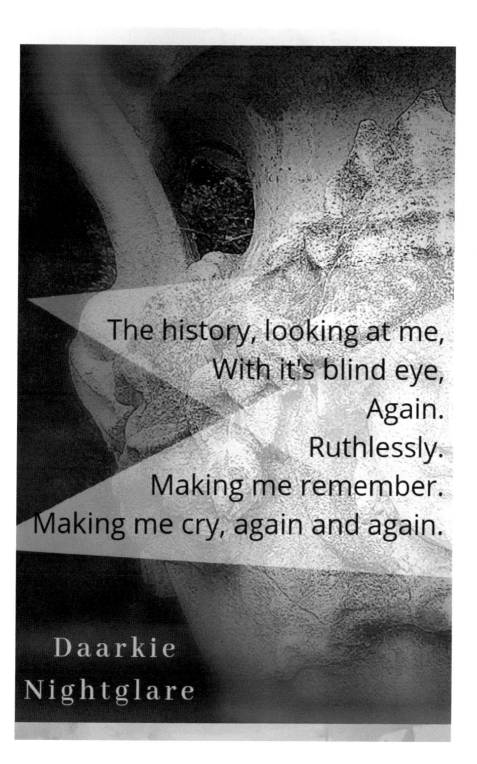

The history, looking at me,
With it's blind eye,
Again.
Ruthlessly.
Making me remember.
Making me cry, again and again.

Daarkie
Nightglare

Daarkie Nightglare

I saw fire in the night,
Little tired, just a bit too bright,
It walked through the forest,
Until it came to stream to rest.

Water simmered in it's wake,
Just as fire came to lake,
Two of opposite sides in world,
Couldn't find the right word.

So, in each other's arms...
They died.

Daarkie Nightglare

Daarkie Nightglare

Daarkie Nightglare

I do believe,
Deep in my soul,
That there's place,
Where I belong.

Đaarkie
Nightglare

35318893R00015

Printed in Great Britain
by Amazon